# *As It Is!*

## *It Is a Body! Can You See It As It Is?*

**A. Sanei, Ph.D.**

*Thanks to all who questioned our answers,*
*those who warned us that more should be done.*

# *Preface*

## *What is This Book About?*

The issues discussed in this book are generally directly related to self-knowledge and self-discovery. The main topic concerns the mind's misconceptions and fallacies that are based on inappropriate assumptions when it attempts to know itself. Specifically, the mind's huge mistake and deep illusion in making no differentiation between the psychological self and physical reality is examined in detail.

As far as the author's research shows, it appears that no book has been published that deals specifically with this issue in such detail. This book tackles the topic in an original manner without becoming involved with unnecessary complexities. Through the simplest analyses and employing the most basic daily experiences, the readers of this text come to know the tricks of their mind in confusing themselves with their physical bodies. This revolutionary and awakening recognition reveals the mind's deepest illusion-making process, and in the end leads the reader to the most authentic and purest knowledge of the self.

The topics of the book are introduced without any predisposition towards a specific philosophy, system of thought, or belief system (non-religious, religious, or anti-religious). Due to the book's objective manner of analysis and offering questions that are completely based on simple daily experiences, the reader's mind will gradually be transitioned to an exceptionally passive observational state, which leaves no room for anything but further contemplation about the discussed issues in inner silence. For this reason, I predict that this discussion will attract a vast variety of readers, and any reader with any intellectual background will be able to follow and understand the arguments. Perhaps it can be said that the book offers twenty-first century readers the smoothest reexamination of the deepest ancient notions in the field of self-knowledge and awareness.

## *Personal Note*

My first meeting with Mr. Jafar Mosaffa in the early Fall of 1986 was perhaps what gave rise to this book. Mr. Mosaffa is the author of, in my opinion, some of the best works in the field of self-knowledge and self-discovery, one of which has been reprinted in Iran more than twenty times. I had just read his books and was very eager to meet him and discuss with him some issues related to self-knowledge. When I did meet him, in Darakeh, north of Tehran, I asked him toward the end of the meeting to teach me an exercise that would help me in my path to self-knowledge. He continued eating his scrambled eggs, and after a moment of silence told me to stop looking at my hand as my hand, and instead to regard it as merely a hand, or rather as *a thing*. From then on, this practice was added to my routine.

One afternoon a few months later, while I was practicing Maharishi's Transcendental Meditation (TM), a spontaneous insight about the visual system appeared in my mind. A combination of this life-changing vision, its results and extension to other areas, gradually created a series of insights and perceptions that radically changed my perspective about my self and its existence.

A short while later, on one of our weekly hikes, I talked about my new insight with Mr. Mosaffa. He asked me to share it with the friends in our hiking group that day and also to talk about it in one of the self-knowledge weekly gatherings that took place at his house in those days. At that time, he was in the final stages of working on his book *The Relationship* and asked me, along with a few others, to read and edit the manuscript before he published it. Realizing his interest in my findings, I summarized them in a few pages, which he was kind enough to include verbatim in his book.

Throughout the years since then, I have discussed these materials with very few people, but have now decided to share part of them with a larger audience in the form of a book. In general, the book is an easy read and does not need any specialized prior knowledge. However, I have no doubt that reading and appreciating the materials will result in radical changes in your perspective and self-consciousness.

This book is divided into two parts. The first part, which includes the topics that have been my main motivation for creating this manuscript, covers the principal ideas. The second part, which can be regarded as a side note or supplement to the first part, discusses some very important topics, although these are not necessarily related directly to the topics presented in the first part. You will notice that the tones of the first and second parts are different. The first part tries to convince you that you need to question your current points of view, and only then seek the answers by yourself. The second part, although it again asks you to discover things by yourself, mainly tries to picture an intuitive experience, rather than asking you to question your reasoning or current points of view.

I would like to emphasize that I do not claim to be a master of self-knowledge or that I have had any extraordinary experiences. I am just an ordinary human being who wants to share some of his thoughts and visions with other human beings.

Take this book as a small gift from me, and I hope you find its contents shocking enough to awaken your mind to see why I have titled *As It Is* as it is!

A. Sanei
California
August 2014

# *As It Is!*

*It Is a Body! Can You See It As It Is?*

*A. Sanei, Ph.D.*

# *Part I*

## *Introduction*

The subjects that will be discussed in this book are closely and directly related to self-knowledge. The question of the relationship between body and mind comprises one of the most important components in many serious texts that tackle the issue of self-knowledge. However, in most of the works previously published in this field, mind and thought have been the main focal points, and the role that the body plays on the path to self-knowledge has been either ignored or not discussed as it should be. In other words, the emphasis has constantly been on the knowing mind and on thought as the product of the mind. In most famous works in the field of self-knowledge, there are multiple definitions of the mind, but no specific definition that pictures the body and clearly distinguishes it from the mind. Many of these works fail to even acknowledge the mind's huge mistake in considering itself to be the same as the body. Correcting this oversight can cause an immensely deep and revolutionary effect on one's perception of self.

In this book, perhaps for the first time, all our attention and energy will be focused on demystifying our illusory description of the body and on delineating the very first step on the path to self-knowledge. We will try to reach conclusions by discussing only completely objective issues, which should be readily understood by any intelligent reader.

The subject of this book concerns the mistiest and vaguest aspects of man's mind; however, the argument is based on ordinary daily observations of the physical world, so the reader does not need to have even an elementary knowledge of any philosophy, religion, thought system, or belief system in order to connect with the discussion in this book.

I am not going to offer you a new belief system or even new knowledge; rather, I am going to ask you to exhaustively examine the authenticity of the assumptions you take for granted. It could be said that this book is about coming to a better understanding of the physics of daily observations, rather than about psychological or mystical issues, although it deals ultimately with the deepest topics discussed in the sphere of self-knowledge.

## *Zero-Point*

"Who am I? What is the self?" These are well-known questions, which have been articulated by many people, famous or not, since antiquity. They occur to almost everyone at one time or another. Many different answers have been offered. Some have many elements in common; others are very different, if not opposite. Every school of thought—religious, irreligious, or anti-religious—has offered its own answer. Except for special cases to be clarified later, all these systems, using their own specific terms, try to describe what the self, the ego, the "I," or personal identity is. For instance, one ideology may deem the self as a collection of evil desires; another may consider it to be the same as the soul; some regard it as a form of memory; still others regard it as a specific level of consciousness. It has also been viewed as a series of complicated procedures in the nervous system, the collection of deeds in previous lives, or a component of universal consciousness.

We will not discuss any of these systems and descriptions or even try to validate or renounce them, simply because our discussion precedes all these discussions regarding logical and analytical arguments. Regardless of the minor or major differences between those thought systems, most of them share a common feature: they attempt to explain what the self or personal identity is. Believing that this is a weakness in those arguments, I instead approach the issue by using a method that can be considered as solving the problem by reversing it.

This reverse approach entails discovering what the self is *not*, rather than focusing on what the self *is*. This, of course, poses enormous new challenges for the mind, but I believe it is the most precise, direct, and effective way to approach the Self Question—that is, the question of "What is self?" or "Who am I?" I believe this approach is the most honest— and therefore the most difficult—way to tackle the issue. You should be ready for severe blows that can destroy the foundations of your conventional perceptions!

In my opinion, the greatest mistake committed in finding the answer to "Who am I?" is that we do not approach the issue free of presumptions and biases. People usually tackle the question by relying on a series of preconceptions, which they believe to be true, and then forward the answers according to those beliefs and presuppositions. It is obvious that if

6

those presuppositions do not have logical foundations or are not compatible with physical facts, they will result in invalid, illogical, and illusory conclusions. By *illusory*, I mean whatever contradicts facts, physical reality, and objective experience.

This discussion will not go beyond the physical laws that govern our daily lives. In fact, there is no need to go beyond those laws. You will find the discussion simple, natural, and tangible. For instance, I do not intend to observe or analyze the findings of quantum physics here. Our discussion throughout the book will be quite simple and remain in the context of daily life. Hence, any mind that is able to observe and comprehend ordinary experiences is all you will need to understand the arguments.

In order to follow the text, you will not need to be a mystic, scientist, physicist, philosopher, or psychologist, or have any extraordinary mental ability. However, as with any question, you will need to be alert and attentive in order to find solutions. Needless to say, an attentive mind is one that has an interest in the issue at hand. In other words, a bit of interest is all you need to start. Fortunately, I can assume that this interest is already there from the fact that you already have the book in your hands. I believe your interest will increase as you continue reading.

In order to avoid oversimplification, let me point out another factor whose presence is required for us to continue forward—for without it, our progress on the path will be slow, if not completely stalled. Lacking this attitude, one would be trapped within old webs of beliefs, which would make it difficult to achieve fresh visions and perceptions. This essential factor is nothing but the courage we must have when we face new perceptions. This factor is not limited to the present discussion, but is an element of every discovery that raises doubts about or even demolishes previous beliefs. Daring to doubt the validity of our beliefs and having the courage to seek new methods are the foundations of any creative and innovative action. I would like to clarify that questioning certain beliefs does not necessarily mean that they are false or that we will inevitably conclude that they will be refuted.

Another subject worth mentioning is that the issues covered in this book, if not foundational themselves, can complement your elementary concepts of self-knowledge. Reading this book and developing even a basic understanding of it will help you to have a deeper appreciation of the teachings of the masters of self-knowledge. However, it is my hope that reading this work will give you such a deep understanding of the self and the world around you that you will be less likely to need the experiences and teachings of others on the path.

## *The Question!*

What is the essence of self, and how is it defined? As I suggested earlier, let us approach this question through finding answers to what the self is not. The reason for choosing this method is that the mind already has preconceived answers, which were conceived and internalized early in life, to the question "Who am I?" What I plan to do is to examine these preconceptions and investigate which ones are invalid. I must emphasize that our goal is not to examine which of these presuppositions is true, but quite the opposite. Trying to approach the question of what the self is *not* will have absolutely different ramifications from asking what the self *is*.

No one can claim that the mind has no answers to the question "What is the self?" The mind creates an image of the self one way or another. Therefore, it makes sense to first examine the validity of this image; otherwise, the mind loses its genuine ability to question its surroundings. We should first discover how we imagine the self in our mind.

As a habit, consciously or unconsciously, the mind does not start from scratch. In any analysis, the mind tends to work based on a series of assumptions; this mechanism creates a blissful ignorance for the mind that commonly prevents any form of creativity and innovation. These presuppositions can be compared to mathematical or geometrical axioms. If these axioms are logically sound, the statements derived from them should be correct; any conclusion based on false starting points will be invalid. The same goes for the mind and its activities. If we try to solve a problem with a mind filled with false suppositions, we will end up with incorrect, untrue, and invalid conclusions. Therefore, we should examine what our starting point is and determine if our axioms are necessary, sufficient, and self-evident.

## Minimum Number of Suppositions

In order to clarify and distinguish our exact starting point, let us first set two ground rules that I consider to be axiomatic. This is a necessary step in establishing any logical statement. First, we assume that it is axiomatic that the physical Universe exists. In other words, we take it for granted that we have no doubt about the existence of the Universe. The essence of this existence, or how it is viewed or should be viewed, is not yet our concern. The only thing we have accepted so far is that the Universe has a physical reality; it has a real existence; it is not nonexistent.

Our second basic supposition is that real creatures, including human beings, or what are considered to be humans at the moment, exist in this Universe. However, despite acknowledging the existence of humans, we have not yet explained or defined what humans are. We have only

11

acknowledged that they exist, and their existence is real. To be more precise, we have not yet clarified if a human being is or is not a soul, spirit, body, ego, or self. It should be obvious by now why I have not attempted to define what human beings are: we want to start from scratch; otherwise, there would be no reason to write this book.

So far, we have acknowledged that the Universe exists in which creatures called human beings exist and are parts of this Universe. But the matter is not as simple as it seems; in fact, a great question arises at this point: How can we perceive this Universe and demonstrate it to others? In other words, how can we understand the way in which we perceive the Universe; and when we do, how can we present our own perception to others?

We have accepted that a Universe exists that is perceivable. But here lies an ambiguity about the essence of this perception in our mind and the reality that exists outside of the human mind in the real World. The difference is not partial and quantitative, but general and essential. The Universe and the human beings that exist are quite different from the universe (with a lower-case *u*) and the human beings perceived by the mind. They are different in essence; that is, the mind's perception of the Universe is merely a processed image, irrespective of what does or does not exist in the real Universe outside the mind. As mentioned earlier, we are not denying the reality of the Universe and its creatures, including human beings, but consider their existence axiomatic. The ambiguity relates to *what* and *how* the mind pictures the Universe. The question is, how authentic is the universe that is built, imagined, or processed in the mind?

It is noteworthy that this mind-made world or universe is not an extraordinary and bizarre concept. It is actually the world or universe as we know it; because the universe that we know is nothing but the universe created by our mind. In fact, each of us has access only to the universe that we have created on our own!

It might seem that we are verging on philosophical issues, but that is absolutely not so. The present discussion is not at all philosophical and abstract, but rather practical and matter-of-fact. As we shall see, it gradually covers the most tangible, most experiential, and most physical aspects of daily life.

## Seeing!

The world, the universe, the cosmos! We have used these words countless times in our life. The general assumption is that people comprehend and demonstrate the meaning of them clearly, completely, and without any problem. But let us ask our question once more: Can you show me the world or universe as you perceive it? Can you really? I will try to explain why the answer to this apparently idiotic question is "No!" But let us first review a few simple facts.

Lift your eyes from this page and look around you. Now try to describe with ordinary language the process and procedures of seeing. A simple explanation of the phenomenon might go as follows: the eyelids are opened, light enters the eyes and stimulates a group of visual cells, which causes a series of electrochemical reactions in the nervous system and brain, and so on. After entering the eye,

15

light is transformed into something else, whose nature is not important for the purposes of this discussion; it can be an electric pulse or a chemical reaction. Whatever it is, it is no longer the light that was emitted or reflected from the object into the eye. Right?

From this point on, we are left in darkness. As soon as the light is transformed into electrochemical reactions, we lose any type of direct relation with what has entered the eyeball. After being created in the eye, that electric pulse moves through the nervous system, reaching the parts of the brain that analyze and process the signals. For the purpose of this discussion, what physiological reactions occur in which parts of the brain do not concern us.

Ultimately, after a series of complex procedures, the brain produces an image—a colored, three-dimensional, super-high-resolution image! This picture is not the physical object. It is just an image created through the brain's activity. It has not been directly created by the optical superposition of the light waves emitted or reflected by the physical object. It has been imagined by the brain and is *essentially* different from what exists out there.

It does not concern us here that this image is deficient because of some sort of physiological shortcoming in the eyes. For example, one such shortcoming might be the filtering mechanism that makes it impossible for the eye to capture the full light spectrum emitted or reflected by the object. Even if the eye did not operate as an electromagnetic filter, which omits a great deal of data, our questions would still remain. What comes to existence in the mind is produced by the visual system and is essentially different from its external counterpart. These two identities come from two different worlds and exist in two different worlds. One is a material object in the physical World, while the other is a mental entity produced through cerebral activity in the personal mental world.

Therefore, when looking at an object, even though we are looking at the same physical entity, what I see is only in *my* mind, and what you see is only in *your* mind; what I see is my mental creation, and what you see is your mental creation. Not only are these two images different from each other, but they also differ from their external corresponding object. So, we are dealing with three distinct entities!

## The Beholder!

People believe, through force of habit, that we are directly watching the external World with our eyes, when in fact we are just seeing what the mind creates inside our mental space. In other words, the images we see with the help of our visual system are not in our eyes, but constructed in our brain and then appear in our mental space. We see only those "images" and have access only to those "images." This is not a poetic interpretation of a mystical secret. It is exactly what actually happens—a factual report of what occurs. Once we acknowledge the essential disparity between the external physical objects and the images created in the mind, we face some subtle questions: Where is the "person" who sees these images? How and with what tool does he or she see? Clearly, there is no eye in the brain or cerebral space, so how and by what are the created images apprehended? Can

19

you show me the beholder in the mind? Can you show the observer of these images to others or even to yourself? Can you find the Cartesian coordination at which this watcher is located?

On a side note, imagine the solitude of the beholder who is sitting in the mental space forced to behold only his or her own mentally created images, content that he or she is seeing the "World," not realizing that he or she has no direct access to the outside, but only to some images of it.

In this discussion, it is not important what does or does not exist outside the mind or how it does or does not look. What matters is the realization that what we see in the process of seeing is just a secondhand creation of the mind. No matter how we interpret the phenomenon of seeing, we do not have any direct understanding of the external world or any immediate access to it. A dark and foggy tunnel separates us from external objects, a tunnel of electrical pulses, and we are at the dark end of it. This fact is horrifying but true. If we contemplate thoroughly, we realize that everything is hazy. Where and how these images are produced, who observes them in the mental space, and how this observation actually occurs are all questions the answers to which are concealed in darkness and ambiguity.

## *I See!*

We use the phrase *I see* automatically and habitually, as in "I see that book." We are not used to questioning the validity of such claims. But is the statement "I see that book" correct? Is it logical and compatible with reality? If I am truly the one who sees, am I able *not to see*? Am I able not to see something in the same way that I am able to see it? Is it possible not to see consciously with my eyes wide open? You know the answer is no. The truth is that the act of seeing is not under the control of "I." Basically, when the eyes are open and the light is sufficient, the act of seeing occurs automatically. In fact, the act of seeing occurs absolutely by itself. If you doubt it, open your eyes and try not to see something! You realize you cannot. So be careful the next time you want to use the phrase *I see*!

That phrase is logically incorrect. It is incompatible with what actually happens and does not explain the phenomenon accurately. The correct statement would be "My eyes see" or "My visual system sees." But, as we will explain later, even this is not the most exact way of conveying the idea. It is best to say, "*The* eyes see" or "*The* visual system sees." Period!

We imagine ourselves to be the agent in the act of seeing, whereas we can neither start nor finish its procedure! It starts automatically with the opening of the eyelids and ends when they are closed. Our will has nothing to do with it. Our presence or absence has nothing to do with it. It is an automatic procedure, regardless of the control or will of the "beholder." The whole feeling of control and agency in relation to seeing is an illusion.

Please note that there are still many ambiguities in our scrutiny of the problem. We have not yet described the person, his (or her) position in the mind, or the manner and means of seeing. For instance, stating that the means of seeing are unclear indicates that we do not know how the mental images are received by the agent. We do not have an extra visual system or extra pair of eyes in the brain. So, which eyes see the images created by the brain? Where are these eyes if we take their existence for granted? Even if we suppose that the beholder has a specific visual instrument for seeing mental images, that will not answer any of our previous questions. In that case, unfortunately, the images perceived in that way would be doubly removed from the physical reality of the external World!

There is an automatic nervous system in the head that transforms light into electricity, which it then transfers through the nerves to the bit of fat that we call the brain. Then, with the help of the electric pulses received from the nerves, the brain creates an image in an unknown space that we are calling the "mental space." Ultimately, a beholder whose location and means of observation are unknown to us finds himself (or herself) watching these images. Or we could more accurately say that the beholder thinks of himself as the observer of the images. In other words, the beholder believes that he is directly observing the physical World, when in fact he is merely seeing the images created by his brain from and inside the mental space. Can you think of any other explanation for this physical phenomenon?

Basically, the "receiver" or the mental person who receives the data is not in direct contact with anything in the external World. By the external World, I mean everything outside the mental space—in which, by the force of a faulty habit, "I" imagines itself as the "beholder," the agent that identifies itself with the eyes or visual system and considers their operation as its own.

This feeling of agency is merely an illusion. The being and non-being of this agent have no influence on the procedure. The visual system does its job independent of the existence or non-existence of the "I." No matter what "I" thinks about its agency, the eyes and other parts of the visual system do their job on their own. The "I" merely has an objective role, whereby it only receives data processed and produced by the visual system.

# *I Hear!*

We use the phrase *I hear* as if it were "I" who hears. But this utterance is based on a false assumption. Let us first start with a simple explanation of hearing and its operation. A mechanical vibration is produced somewhere in the environment. Then its energy, in the form of a sound wave, is transferred to our ears through a material medium, and vibrates certain parts inside the ear. This vibration creates a series of electrical pulses that are transferred through nerves to specific parts of the brain. Ultimately, the brain processes these pulses, creating a feeling—or we might better say an illusion—of hearing.

Interestingly, in reality, we do not hear the external sound, but the sound created by our brain. There are no sounds outside the brain, only waves and vibrations. Every brain creates its own sounds independent of and different from those created by other brains. When several people hear a single sound, the brain of each of them creates its own unique mental sound independently and without any mental or physical link to the other brains. Every person hears the sound of his or her own brain, not the sound created outside, and not the sound produced by the other brains there. Each brain creates its own sounds and then hears them!

Can you locate where the sound is produced in the brain and show that location to others? Where in the brain is the sound created? Where in the brain is it heard? Who hears and feels the sound in the brain? Where is the hearer who comprehends the sound after its creation? How and with what tools does the hearer hear? With another pair of ears?!

Can you initiate or end the process of hearing at will? Can you *not hear*? Can you hear? Is it *you* who does the act of hearing? Or are you involuntarily forced to hear what your ears hear?

The truth is, just as the eyes see automatically, the ears hear automatically. They do not need your will or wish or even your attention to do so. In fact, instead of saying, "I hear," you should say, "My ears hear." Actually, the most accurate description would be to say, "*The* ears hear." Period!

The eyes see and the ears hear automatically, independently, and without needing "me," whether or not "I" need to do something special to make them see or hear. Knowing and experiencing these truths frees the mind from the everlasting burden of the two heavy duties of seeing and hearing! You don't need to do anything; they are done, and they always have been done! Even thinking about this fact brings a certain lightness and freedom to the mind. Can you feel this relief?

## *It Touches!*

As a complement to our discussion about seeing and hearing, it might be helpful to discuss the sense of touching. You probably know what I am about to say. Let us examine what actually happens in the act of touching. How does it start and how is it fulfilled? The first thing that happens is that the skin comes into contact with something. That contact is converted by the skin into electrochemical data that is transferred by the nerves to the brain. It is not the "person," or what is referred to as the "person," who touches; it is the skin that touches. My "I" does not touch anything, but my skin does. Right?

Then the brain processes this data and produces the feeling of touching or being touched. Similar to seeing and hearing, what is felt in the mind is a secondhand recreation that is essentially different from what actually happens in the physical touch between the skin and the object. What I perceive as the roughness of a surface is a feeling created by my brain, and is felt in my mental space, not where it actually takes place.

There is a vague space between me and that touch, and, as mentioned earlier, it is not clear how "I" feels this touch and through what means. Is that not so?

## The Mental Space

To sum up, everything we see and hear is in our minds, and we cannot have a direct and unmediated understanding of the World. We see and hear, but it all takes place in the confined and vague space of the mind. We are a prisoner of our mind and have access only to what is provided for us in this prison. That is a fact. Moreover, we do not really know where the "I" who receives these visual and auditory products is located. We do not know how this "I" receives these audio-visual products and data. It is not clear how our "I" sees or hears.

Our "I" seems to be somewhere in the dark and vague space of the mind, but it cannot be located—that is, we don't know where we are! Where is this person, the "I," consciousness, or self-consciousness? Where and in which spot is it located? Where is the receiver of the brain's data?

31

Where and how does the "I" receive the data? Is it basically correct to use the word *where* for this consciousness? Is this "receiver" locatable at all? These are seminal questions, to which we do not have clear answers. Is that not so?

Have you ever tried to feel your mental space? Have you ever tried to find it inside you? Or better yet, have you ever tried to find yourself in this space? If you think about it, the mental space cannot be pinpointed, referred to, or positioned; its location and dimension are vague; nothing is known about it.

It might be said that the space is created through electrochemical reactions in the brain cells, or at least a feeling of it is produced. Even if we accept this explanation, has anything been clarified? Does this ambiguous answer help us to solve anything?

It is not clear what the essence of our mental space is and what its limitations are or are not. Can or can't it be physically measured? Can it even really exist? It might be just a fantasy, an illusion, like a dream. Try to find and feel this strange space through meditation and contemplation in silence and solitude. Where exactly is the place that you locate yourself? Even if you find its location, can you give any hint of its whereabouts to others?

## *A Lonely Spectator; Only One Spectator!*

We can rewrite these bizarre stories about any perception we have of the external World. In all cases, a dark, vague, irremovable, and unavoidable space exists between, on the one hand, the actual external World and, on the other, the mental consciousness of the "I" who is the final receiver of the processed data. Our observations are not direct and firsthand, but internal productions; the brain creates them for us; therefore, we can perceive only what the brain has created, not the actual reality out there. It does not matter how similar the mental image is to the external object. This is not that. Period!

As a side note, in the case of hearing, for example, even the supposition that the brain recreates sound is incorrect, because no sound actually exists in the physical World. It might be possible to claim for vision that the brain somehow recreates the images of external realities, but that is not true for sound. The brain somewhat creates sound. To be more precise, the brain creates the hearing experience independent of the external World; the creation of a mental sensation is quite different from the re-creation of a real physical external entity. The same goes for some other issues, such as colors. As these issues are not the concern of this discussion, however, I will not pursue this matter any further.

Ultimately, it is my brain that creates the whole universe for me! By "my brain" I mean nothing other than that mass of fat in my skull! It is my brain that visualizes a complete world and screens it for me like a movie in a theatre. This is a single-spectator theatre, in which I am the only one present. Furthermore, my theatre is isolated from the external World, as well as from other theatres; there is no direct link among them. The scenes screened at these theatres might be about a common subject, but each theatre shows its own unique movie for its own single spectator. The spectators are isolated from one another and condemned to sit in their solitude, watching their own creations. What we conceive as "our surroundings" are nothing but scenes in this movie!

Each person has his or her own mind and his or her own world. None of these worlds is what lies out there. What is out there is real and authentic, and what is in the mind is just a self-made image—an illusion that makes us mistake a picture for the real thing.

34

Another subtle point that I am trying to make here is that the aforementioned conclusions are extended to other people just as much as to everything else in the self-made universe of the mind. This verdict applies to them, too! Those mental persons are not excluded from these conclusions. The people whose existence I feel in my mind are not the ones in the real world. They are creatures of my mind; I think them; I imagine them; my mind fancies them. These characters are of my own making. I am facing characters who have been created by my own brain and my own nervous system; my brain's processor has produced them. The person I observe is not the same as that actual being who lives out there.

Not only understanding, accepting, and "knowing" this fact, but even comprehending it logically and analytically poses a great shock to the human psyche. I meet and contact different people every day; I live with them; they have physical reality out there; but I am not in contact with those realities. This is one of the fundamental issues to which I will return later.

## Breathing

Having discussed seeing, hearing, and touching, it is time to discuss another important bodily experience—that is, breathing. The case of breathing is quite interesting because we are constantly doing it. It is always with us, day and night, asleep or awake, sitting or walking; in short, whether we are doing something or not doing anything at all, we breathe. Other activities might be interrupted by short or long intervals; but breathing is continuous; it starts from the moment of birth and continues constantly up till the final moment of life. The body stops living as soon as breathing stops. A person might be blind or deaf, but cannot be short of an active respiratory system. Therefore, "breathing" should be discussed in detail.

## *I Breathe!*

Let us examine the process of breathing precisely. You believe that you are the one doing the breathing. You believe that you are the one inhaling and exhaling and keeping this continuous flow. You feel that if you stop breathing, the process will stop, and you will face problems. Is it not so? Do you think or feel otherwise? If so, naturally you should feel that the air is inhaled and exhaled automatically, without requiring your participation. But most probably you do not feel that, no matter what your logic and reasoning may tell you. Most probably, you feel that you are the one doing the breathing, the constant inhaling and exhaling procedure.

However, it is interesting to note that we have this sense of agency and active presence in the process so long as we are paying attention to breathing. But as soon as we think about something else or go to sleep, for example, we do not have the feeling that we need to do the breathing. In other words, we never feel the need to willfully breathe and continue breathing when we are not conscious of it.

What is the source of this contradiction? Why don't we have a problem when we are not paying attention to our breathing, but as soon as we become conscious of it, we feel an urge to breathe, fearing that otherwise our breathing will stop and we will suffocate?

Stop breathing for a few seconds willingly in order to see your mind's reaction and the strong sense you have of the necessity of *active* breathing. We experience the necessity of willfully inhaling and exhaling as soon as we consciously start to think about them; as if it were us doing the breathing, and if we stopped, everything would collapse, resulting in our death!

The interesting point is that we need to do something *not to breathe*, but we don't need to do anything to breathe! Breathing can occur automatically, and it does so most of the time, whether we are conscious of it or not. The illusion that I am breathing results in a disruption of its natural and automatic flow. It is interesting to see how a mere act of directing attention to breathing transforms it from an automatic act into one that appears to be intentional. When we are not attentive to our breathing—for instance, when we are busy with our chores or are sleeping—we do not feel the need to control our breathing, nor is there any need for such control.

The truth is that "I breathe" is as absurd as "I see." "I" is not breathing! "Breath is breathed," and "I" does not have any role in it. Breathing was there from the instant we were born, when self-awareness in the form of "I" was not yet formed. It has always been and continues to be in sleep, in wakefulness, and in all of our everyday experience without any need for our presence or control. It is a fallacious belief to consider yourself the "breather." There is no breather! The body does the breathing by itself and has no need for your interference or even your presence.

There is also a misconception about the physics of breathing. We believe that we draw air into the lungs through the nose or mouth when we inhale, and blow it out when we exhale. This is completely wrong and one of the funniest misconceptions of the mind, which tricks us into believing such a notion. In reality, no air is drawn in by the nose or mouth. What actually happens is that the expansion of the lungs creates a difference in air pressure that causes the air to enter the lungs automatically. That is, the mouth, the nose, and even the lungs have no pumping role in inhaling; what happens is that the lungs are expanded, and then the air automatically enters that expanded space. In fact, it is the external air pressure that pushes the air into the nose, and not the suction power of the mouth or nose to draw air in. Compare this actual physical procedure of breathing to our ordinary assumption! Isn't it funny?

In order to get a better understanding of the issue, try to experience the real process of breathing as it happens

41

automatically, free from illusions. Sit—or preferably, lie down—and try to experience breathing as it really occurs. You will soon realize that this is not an easy task, because the mind vehemently resists the fact that breathing is done by itself! The conscious mind stubbornly wants to control the process of inhaling and exhaling; it does not want to accept that, a few moments earlier, breathing was done automatically. We are not ready to stop breathing so easily!

What is the source of this resistance? Why should it be so hard for the mind to consciously leave this automatic process alone, even for a moment? This question can arise with every breath we take. Ask yourself this question tonight with every breath you take, when you are lying in your bed, ready to go to sleep. Feel your mind's resistance to leave breathing as it is; watch its fear of letting go; sense its bizarre and irrational fear of automatic breathing. What do you think is the reason behind this fear?

## *Hand, Foot, Body!*

The point I will discuss in this section concerns another internalized misconception about the body and its relationship to the mind. Deep down in the mind, we feel that the "self" is what keeps the body whole and maintains its integrity and continuity. Our intuition tells us that "I" am the reason for the existence and survival of my body. We think the body exists because I exist, whereas logically it should be the other way around. That is, I exist because this body exists. Right? First, there is the "body," and then my self-consciousness, my presence, my sense of existence, and the sense that I am here.

Before going ahead, I think this is a good time to mention a golden technique that you will find amazingly useful on your path to self-knowledge. I learned it from Mr. Mosaffa, who later asked me to consider it the most important self-

43

knowledge exercise during my normal daily activities. It simply is this: Imagine yourself out of your physical body, looking at it from a distance. This includes the body and the content of the mind—as if you were looking at a stranger, to whom you don't have any specific feeling. It is like looking at yourself as "him" if you are a man, or looking at yourself as "her" if you are a woman. Having a "him-ness" or "her-ness" vision about yourself might be a good name for this exercise. This is a highly beneficial and incredibly enlightening exercise that you may wish to practice whenever you feel aware of yourself, or anytime you remember it. This excellent exercise can be done in any physical or emotional situation: talking, walking, sitting, watching, running, lying, laughing, crying, arguing, hating, loving, and so on. This looking can be at the body as a whole, or focused on some part of it; for example, your hand, leg, eye, ear, face, and so on. This golden technique will help you to see yourself as you are!

It appears to be an easy exercise, but it is actually a very difficult one. We don't want or like to look at ourselves. In fact, we hate it! Furthermore, we don't like people who try to show us to ourselves or even ask us to look at ourselves! You may need to put great time and effort into mastering this priceless exercise. Stop blaming yourself if you want to master it quickly! You do understand why, right?

As I asked above, try to imagine yourself out of your body, looking at it from outside. Now tell me if the statement "This body is there because I am there" really has a logic to it? Does the "I" need to be at a place or time in order for the body to be at that place or time? Does my body need me in order to be? Isn't it true that most of the time "I" am not there, but my body is still there; for instance, when I am deeply asleep or immersed in my thoughts? Does the body need the conscious presence of the "I" in these moments in order to "be"?

Our mental sense is that not only am "I" the reason behind the integrity of the body, but the body as a whole is the same as "I," as though if I did not exist, my body would cease to exist. In other words, "I" exist in different parts of the body and ensure its being and survival and continuity. As with our discussion of the procedure of breathing, the illusion of agency shows itself when we focus on the body or one of its parts; as if this body did not exist a moment ago and has just come into existence in its whole form through our attention!

Existence or non-existence of the physical body is not under your control or will. It exists by itself. Whether "you" exist or not, your hands, feet, ears, and eyes exist without needing you to fasten yourself to them! The beingness or non-beingness of the body and its limbs are independent of our will and control. There is no need for "I" in order for the body to exist. Basically, there never has been any need for it to maintain the physical existence of this pile of flesh. Can you feel the existence of your physical body, here at this moment, as an entity independent of your mental being? Can you feel the dissociation of your body from your mind?

Can you feel the urge, the irrational urge, to attach yourself to your body?

In order to relate to the issue more deeply, lie down in silence and pay attention to your body and your sense of it. You probably feel that your body exists because you exist. That is, you exist first, and then comes the body. You feel that its being here depends on you, and not the other way around. You feel that you contain and hold it, and not that the body contains and holds you. You also feel that you are inside your body. For instance, when you pay attention to your hand, your sense is that the hand is a part of "you." You feel that the existence of this hand depends on your existence. It seems impossible and incomprehensible to you that this hand is there, whether or not "you" exist! You feel that this hand is a part of you, a part of what is called your "I." But is that really so?

I will answer on your behalf: definitely not! For the simple reason that when you avert your attention from your hand to other things, the hand still remains without feeling any change! Your hand—your whole body in fact—is still there without needing you to be with it or to carry it everywhere. Actually, it is not you who carries the body; it is the body that carries you here and there! Can you see that?

Our thoughts and thinking habits are resistant to such a simple and clear fact. Your mind wants to believe that this is your body, and that that body is here because you are here. Do you see the difference? Under the pressure of habit, the

46

mind cannot—even does not want to—accept this fact and leave the body alone! Can we make the mind accept the simple logic of existential independence of the body? Can we lie down for a moment and completely let the body alone? Can you really accept that this body lying in bed does not need you to hold so fast to it? It does not seem to be easy and simple. Right?

After reading this text, we may want to try to let the body go, as if it were constrained thus far, and now we should try to set it free! We are blind to the fact that the body does not cling to us; we cling to the body. At least, when we are asleep, the body is lying there and does not need to be detached from us! It is quite bizarre that the mind finds it difficult to acknowledge such straightforward facts. "I" has difficulty accepting the simple truth that the body can be here and there without the "I" needing to imagine that it is "my body."

## *Imaginary vs. Physical Reality*

If the body is autonomous and already detached from us, what makes us believe that we are the ones holding it and clinging so tightly to it? How is it that we feel we are in the body's head, hand, and foot and cannot leave it even for a second? Why do we desperately feel that we have to try hard to release the body? What is the reason behind this absurd mental habit?

The truth is that the body we "feel" in our mind has nothing to do with the real physical body. We have created a mental body for ourselves, a mere mental image that we mistake for the real thing; we mistake this for that and consider them to be the same. It is an illusion, a huge mistake.

There is a hand in the real World, but it also has a counterpart in our mind, which we mistakenly take for the

49

real one attached to our body. These two hands are different and independent entities. Whether or not I am paying attention to my mental hand at this particular moment, the real one exists in the external World. The mental hand is an image, a mental image. We have no direct link to the real hand. The hand that we feel is the one created in the mind; it is there for one minute and disappears the next. But the real hand is autonomous, always there in the external World. Its beingness or non-beingness does not depend on the beingness or non-beingness of the imagined hand. Even if the imagined hand disappears forever, the real one will still exist without feeling any difference; in fact, it does not care about my or anybody else's imaginations or illusions! Even if the owner of that imaginary hand dies, the real one still exists, attached to the body, dangling from the body, until it decays and slowly rots—and, of course, again by itself!

Extend this example to the whole body. The body exists in the external World, whether "I" do or not. The body is there by itself, whether you are or are not there; it is autonomous in every situation and does not need to be held or set free by you. The release you try to achieve for the body is merely a mental activity that is related to the mental body created in the mind. Maybe we should think of our body in the same sense that we think of our shirt. We never think that we are the one giving life to the shirt or securing its survival. We never try to release it in our mind! The shirt is there! It is released and free, not caring how much we believe it is us or we are it.

Similarly, the body, the physical body, is out there by itself. Like the shirt, the body is not a part of your "I." It is always there, whether you are asleep or awake, whether you are paying attention to it or are completely ignorant of it. This body is out there doing its job, and does not care about you or your attention or inattention. It breathes, sees, hears, laughs, walks, sits, eats, sleeps, and wakes up!

## Just a Body!

Now let us ask another question—a fundamental question that is harder to understand than to answer. The question is quite simple and does not need complex philosophical or scientific deliberations to be understood. The question is, "Can you show me yourself?"

Imagine you are Mr. X or Ms. Y; that is, imagine that you consider yourself to be Mr. X or Ms. Y. Can you show me this Mr. X or Ms. Y? I want to see this Mr. X or Ms. Y! What is your reaction to this demand? You might consider it to be a ridiculous question, or think the answer is quite simple: I am here! Come and see! I am standing right here!

Unfortunately, this answer could not be further from the truth. What you try to show me—that is, what is in front of me—is not you; what I see before me is not Mr. X, it is only

53

his body. What is shown to me is just an object, a body, a pile of flesh, bone, and fat! What I am looking at has nothing to do with your "you." That thing before me is merely a body. What does it have to do with your "self" or your personality? What does this pile of flesh and bones have to do with your identity?

I agree that the body manifests actions and sounds that are the result of your thoughts and mental activity. This, however, is not that. Imagine that a person is standing before you. The "thing" you consider to be the "person" is actually a collection of limbs and organs with specific functions. In that "thing," each limb and organ receives a certain type of data from its surroundings, transfers that to the brain, which in turn processes it and presents it to us in an unknown space.

The point is that these organs—ears, eyes, nose, hands, and feet—are not the same as your "self" or your "I." Hands and feet are merely some flesh and bones, nothing more. Moreover, what I see in front of me is not even your hands and feet, but just hands and feet! It is true that those hands and feet are under your control, but being under your control does not add anything more to them. In the final analysis, these are hands and feet that are attached to the brain through some nerve cells. It does not matter how you want to define the body. It does not make any difference what my definition of your "I" is. It does not matter whether or not this body contains an "I." The fact is that my eyes do not see a self in this corpse; It just sees a body. Is that clear?

No matter what thought system you believe in or deny, the result is the same. You might be a materialist or believe in metaphysics or the existence of life after death. It does not matter if you believe that this body has or does not have an astral body or soul related to it. What you see—or rather, what your eyes see—is a hand, a foot, a pile of flesh and bones, a body. In short, objects! Your eyes do not see a self in this corpse; they just see a body. The logic of the matter is quite simple, but it is not easy to make the mind accept it!

No matter what the reasons are behind this resistance, it seems that I cannot see the body as just a body, without attaching the phantom of a self to it! I should be able to see the body as it really is—without labels, identities, or characteristics ascribed to it—free from the "person" who is created by my mind.

Let's try a simple exercise. Stand in front of a mirror and look at it. What do you see? Given our discussion thus far, it should be clear to you that you only see a body. You do not see a "self," but just a body, a pile of flesh and bones. Pay attention! What you see in the mirror is different from what you conceive as your self or identity. The mirror does not show you the "I" who receives brain-processed data that is located or floating in the mental space. What you see in the mirror is a corpse that moves and sometimes makes sounds. Please note that we do not want to talk about the essence of personal identity here; what matters at this point is that whether or not your body carries an identity, your eyes cannot see it. They only see a body! I should emphasize that what your eyes see is not even the body of a person, but just a body, a mass of flesh and bones. Can you see the difference?

You might agree in theory with what has been discussed here, but in practice, when you are looking at a body, you may still see a person. You might say that you even see "the person of that body" before seeing "the body of that person." It seems the problem is still there. Let us go deeper and examine more details.

## *Imaginary Illusionists*

At this point, I suppose that we have logically accepted that our eyes merely see a body rather than a person. But as expected, in practice and under the force of habit, we still feel the presence of a person before us, rather than a mere body. The question is, *Where* is that person whose presence we feel right after observing that body? Where does *he* or *she* come from? How is this sense of presence created and materialized? How is it that as soon as I look at that body, a person—a specific person—comes to life in my mind? I see *my father* when I see *my father's body*. Where on Earth is this "my father"? Where in this Universe? Where is the person who seems to be attached to that body? What is the essence and reality of this identity, which seems to be an inseparable part of that body, dominating it and making it invisible?

Bearing in mind our earlier discussions, it is clear that, for example, my friend, Mr. X, has his own identity or self, which resides in his mind. My friend—I mean his self—is a receiver of data, which, like a vague mass of clouds, flows in his mental space, whatever definition that space may have. But when I talk about him, I am not referring to that mental creature; I am referring to his body; that is, my natural sense is used to working that way. Habitually, when we talk about a person, we have the image of the physical creature in mind. Furthermore, we do not have any direct access to the "person" residing in that individual's mind. So, what is the source of such a conception? What makes that "person" someone I know and whose actual presence I feel? What is the essence of this specific "person," whose presence I feel whenever I look at that particular body?

As with all our previous questions, the answer to this one is simple, but accepting and acknowledging it is hard. The answer is that the person I associate with that specific body exists only in *my* mind. It has been processed and created in my mind alone. My "my father" is nowhere to be found except in my mind; it is my creation. It is an entity processed and defined internally in the seclusion of my mind. Our previous discussions should make the logic behind this issue clear. My father and I create each other! I live with a father who is my own creation, and he lives with a son he has created himself!

The "father" I feel in my mind has nothing to do with the "myself" he feels in his mind. These two "people" are two separate mental entities with nothing in common. They are two different things that have derived from different sources; they are the results of two different processes executed by two different processors. My specific acquaintance, who exists in my mind, has been created by my mind and is exclusively the result of my mental activity. This is a truth that can radically change humanity's view of the world and the self. Let us elaborate the matter more thoroughly.

Imagine that a person, "Mr. X," is in contact with ten different people—friends, family, and colleagues. All of these people have a unique image of Mr. X individually created in their minds. These ten mental identities or persons are different from one another, not just in details but, more importantly, in essence. It is noteworthy to realize that these ten entities are *separate* from each other; their existence and being are not connected or even related. They have nothing in common with the person's conception of himself either, because each image is the result of the work of a different processor.

The reason I keep repeating and emphasizing the distinctness of these mental images is to penetrate the mind's habit of assuming that all these creations are the same, which everyone accepts without question. Each and every one of these ten people who see Mr. X—or actually, his body—see only their own created person, mistakenly thinking that they are looking at the actual self of that body. Each one thinks that the others see or conceive the same person as he or she does—an illusion that has no counterpart in reality. None of these people is able to grasp the sense that the others have of that person; the sense that merely exists in their own mind.

Now let us return to our earlier question: Can you show me your "self"? Or, let me twist the question a bit: Can you show your "self" even to yourself? Hopefully, you are not thinking of using a mirror! It can't help you! As you know, what you see in the mirror is not *you*, but some flesh and bones. And you know what flesh and bones are! If you do not, go to a butcher shop and touch, squeeze, and examine some meats and bones closely. Meat, flesh, bones, and skin are exactly those *things* that you are looking at in the butcher shop; there is nothing more to them than what meets the eyes! This is not only true for you, but for all the people you know. What you consider to be a person and his or her identity in your mind is not the creation of your visual system and has nothing to do with it! Your eyes can only see the body of your mother, father, sister, brother, friends, acquaintances, and colleagues. The rest is the result of your creative mind!

Even more interestingly, what you consider to be *you*, what you conceive as your *self*, has nothing to do with what others see of you. They just see a pile of moving flesh and bones. What they see when they look at you, and what you see in the mirror, is only a body—flesh and fat covering some pieces of bone!

## Behind Your Eyeballs? In Your Brain?

You might say it is true that I only see a body in the mirror, but I am somewhere *inside* this body. You might specifically say, I am *inside the brain.* I am in my brain. Very well, but have you ever seen a brain up close? Go and find yourself a brain and look at it carefully. You do not necessarily need a human brain; that of a cow or sheep will do for this purpose. Look at it carefully and pay attention to its details. Examine the brain carefully and tell me if you can really call that *thing* "myself" or even a bearer of a *self*? Biology tells us that the brain is a network of interconnected neurons. But what is this network of interconnected neurons made of? Excluding water, this network of interconnected neurons is mostly made of fat cells. Then, and also to put it more crudely, let's think of it as just a piece of fat!

If you still think that you are the brain or inside it, try to locate yourself there. Where in this thing are you? In which part of it is your "me" located? Where do you feel your "self" in it? Where in this piece of fat? If you find this task difficult, at least try to discover in which parts you are not! Where is your self, your identity, or your self-awareness in this pile? Where is it not?

You might say that the sense of self-awareness is the result of neural communications in a neural network. However, this explanation is too vague to clarify anything; it evades the real issue, let alone the fact that this explanation has not been scientifically proven yet and lacks a strong and solid basis. Furthermore, even if we accept this explanation, nothing has been resolved, because it is not yet clear where the self or consciousness resides, how it should be defined, and how it emerges and develops. Furthermore, we still face the undeniable fact that the brain before us on the table or the one in the skull is merely a bit of fat, and not a person! Whatever else we see in the brain is the creature of the brain, and not the work of the visual system.

Another common mistake is that we habitually and by default locate our "self" somewhere in the head behind the eyes. We feel the "self" is there; we feel *our location* to be somewhere behind the eyes. If you close your eyes now and try to locate yourself in your body, you will probably find it in your head, behind the eyeballs.

But is this mental sense correct, logical, trustworthy, and compatible with physical facts? Or is it merely an illusion rooted in habit? Have you ever asked yourself what is behind the eyes inside the brain, and what it consists of? Have you ever seen that part of your body up close? If you do not have access to a human brain or head, you can examine the brain or head of a sheep or cow or pig. Take a look at the space behind the eyeballs; that is exactly where we imagine the self to be! Look at that space up close. Is there anything besides fat and flesh there? You will not say, "I am there" if you closely examine what lies there.

The reason behind the assumption that we feel the self behind the eyes might be the importance of the eyes in connecting the internal world with the external World. But then, how do the blind, who lack a working visual system, feel the self? Through their ears? Actually, it doesn't matter. The truth is that we are not behind our eyes or our ears; in fact, we are in no limb or organ of the body. It is only through habit and repetition that we feel we are *in* the body and that we *are* the body. We have gotten used to the idea of seeing the self as the body, in the body, and in its organs. It is time to ask ourselves a meticulous yet scary question: Where exactly in the body am I? Which part does the feeling of being inside the body indicate? *Where* in *this body* do you find yourself?

If you pursue these questions seriously, you will find that you do not have a clear answer to them. If we examine each organ carefully, we find it impossible to locate the "self" in

63

any of them. Where do *I* really reside in this body? The hands, feet, neck, shoulders, back, skull, or stomach? What do these organs consist of? Can you trace the "self" in them? Is there anything besides flesh, bones, and fat? Our body and its parts are not that much different from the flesh, bones, and fat you find in any butcher shop. What is the difference between that meat and the flesh of your body? Why do you see that meat as meat, but see this flesh as the "I"? Why?

The body is just a body. The body is not the "I." The "I" is not the body. The self or "I"—or to be more precise, the sense of self-consciousness or self-awareness—does not and cannot exist in any body part or organ. The body receives information from its surroundings, processes it, and then delivers it to the "I," the receiver. Then everything is lost in a vague darkness. Can we locate the ultimate receiver who watches the processed data? Can we even "describe" it? It seems *unnatural* to our mind, but we do not have a choice other than to accept the fact that we are not in the body. We are not and cannot be anywhere in the body. Where, then, is my "I"?

## *These Eyes? These Eyeballs?*

To continue with our questions, let us ask another one that problematizes our common beliefs. Stand before someone and look at him (or her). You feel that what is standing in front of you is a person—for instance, a friend. If someone asks you what you are looking at, you will say, "I am looking at my friend." The question is, Which part are you referring to when you say, "I am looking at my friend" or "This is my friend"? In which part of his body do you find your friend? Which part exactly contains your friend? Which part of that body does your mind perceive as your friend? His hands? His feet? His stomach? His back? His neck? His ears? His fingers? His teeth? His knees? His eyes?

I am almost certain that your answer will be "his eyes." That is, when we look at someone, we find him in his eyes. We locate him in the eyes and nowhere else. We find his personhood and identity in his eyes, rather than, for example, in his ears, arms, or neck. By default, we regard looking at someone's eyes as the same as looking at "him" or "her."

But what is really the difference between the fat in the eyeballs and the fat in other parts of his body? Is there any essential difference between the eyes, ears, neck, and nose that leads you to seeing people only in their eyes? If you think there is a real difference that justifies your habit, explain it to me! Just bear in mind that you should start your analysis from the premise that the eyeballs consist of a bit of fat and muscle. If you start from this point, you will see that you really cannot justify this habit. The truth is that such a difference does not exist in the real World!

In this context, there is no difference between the eyes and other organs in the physical body. There is no difference between the eyeballs and, for instance, the earlobes or nose. It is merely our mind that makes us picture the body in this way. It has gotten used to—or has been forced by social conditioning to get used to—making this distinction. The person you find standing before you is not in his arm or foot or the fat of his eyes!

We differentiate between a person's eyes and other parts of his or her body, based on a groundless habit. We put too much value on the eyes; as if the *person* resided in the eyes and nowhere else. We make a twofold mistake: first, we consider the body to be the same as the person; and second, we limit this person to the eyes. That is, we do not associate the whole body with the "self." We do not see people in their ears, nose, neck, or knees, but in their eyes, and only in their eyes. When we talk to other people, we talk to their eyes as if they were only their eyes. We do not have the same feeling about their noses, ears, knees, or hands. We do not talk to those; we do not address those parts. We have gotten used to addressing only those two balls of fat and to deeming only those *things* as our audience!

Examine an eye closely and look at its detail. If you can, cut it up and take a look inside. Again, you do not need a human eye; that of a sheep will do! Who can deny that the eye is anything but a white ball that contains some liquid and fat? Is it otherwise? If so, then what is it? Have you ever seen and touched an eyeball? Has it ever occurred to you to look at an eye only as an eye and not as a person? Can you look at someone's eyes without seeing a person in them? Is that gentleman or lady really in the eyeballs, in which you have been locating him or her with such certitude all these years?

Not only do we feel that we are looking at somebody when we look at his or her eyes, but we also feel that a "person" is looking at our "self" when he or she looks at our body. But is that really so? Is this feeling compatible with the facts? A pair of eyes is looking at a body, but we think a person's self is looking at my self.

What actually happens is that his (or her) "self" is *looking at the image of my body in his own mind.* But this is different from saying that his eyes, small balls of fat in a hollow space in his skull, are looking at my "I." Furthermore, that ball of fat is not looking at me, but my body—or more precisely, the image of my body created in his mind. My "I" is somewhere other than he believes. "I" am neither in my body nor in the liquid of my eyeballs. We are not under the surveillance of others as much as we think we are!

## *At Least Let the Dead Alone!*

A funny thing about our last discussion is that not only do we see animate objects as people, but we do so for lifeless bodies as well! Our mind cannot even see the corpses of the dead as they really are. It sees a corpse as if the person is still in there! It seems natural for us to see the body, at least after death, as a lifeless piece of flesh. But we know it is not so. We see *a person* even when we are looking at his or her corpse.

For instance, if the facial muscles of the corpse give the impression of a frown, a smile, or pain, we feel that it is the person who is still frowning or smiling or in pain! It is difficult for the mind to accept that the person is not there, so that the impression left on the face is the result of muscular expansion or contraction of some flesh on some bones. The mind cannot see the flesh, but insists on seeing a person. We can see another example of this when we notice that the fingers of the corpse are clenched, and feel that it is the person who has made a fist. But is what the mind feels real? Or are the fingers merely some bones positioned in a specific way? We do not leave the person alone, even now that he (or she) is dead. "He" is gone; let him be!

But what is the reason for this habitual resistance? At least, now that the person is dead, he should not be seen in this light. But why do we still see him there? As discussed earlier, this self-made "he" is in the mind of the beholder and has always been there. Therefore, it should not surprise us that this "he" is still alive in the mind of the beholder, who has habitually attached this mentally self-made "he" as a tag to that fleshy face. Actually, the beholder's mind is not committing a new mistake, but repeating its original one. The mind cannot conceive of death in that face. The "living being" that the beholder's mind sees in that face has been present and living only in the mental space of the beholder. Therefore, it is natural that the death of that living body should have no special effect on how the mind views it.

## *There Is No One on the Street!*

Go to a place where people are moving around. Observe the scene carefully and describe what you see. What is the most exact answer you can give? The most common answer is that there are persons who are walking around. But is that really the right answer? What is the clearest, most accurate, and simplest answer to this question?

The truth is that you do not see anyone there; you only see the bodies, the moving bodies that move around and make sounds. There are bodies there, but there is nobody there. There, you see the body, but not anybody!

In reality, there is absolute silence there! It is your mind that is making all these noises. I am not talking about literal noise and silence, but simply suggesting that no one is out there. At least, what you see are not "people."

71

What you see there, what your visual system sees, are wandering skeletons, robots made of bones covered with flesh. That is all! You know very well that there is nothing more to it! The rest is all in your mind! Those persons have all been created in that unknown space of the mind we discussed earlier. The scene we are looking at, the street we are walking on, is empty of people! What a scene! What a silence!

By saying this, I do not mean that there are *no* human beings in the World, but I also don't want to say that there *are* human beings in the World. These issues are not my concern at the moment. What I am highlighting now is that whether or not the existence of human beings and their personal identities are real or merely illusions, our conclusions remain the same. In many mystical and self-knowledge systems, the self is considered to be an illusion. There are also other thought systems with different views. However, for the purposes of this discussion, it does not make any difference in which system of thought you do or do not believe. For example, it does not make a difference whether or not you believe in the existence of life after death. The conclusions of this discussion are independent of any of these presuppositions and precede all of them. No matter what system of thought you follow, you cannot ignore the simple and basic fact that what you see on the street are not people but bodies! This is a logically grounded statement that goes beyond any philosophical view about the definition of the essence of mankind.

Whether or not you believe the ego exists, whether or not you believe that ghosts exist, whether or not the ego resides in the brain, whether or not the self is the same as the soul, whether or not you believe in a metaphysical world, or whatever else you may or may not believe makes no difference to the fact that what your eyes see on the street is only the march of bodies, of figures, of piles of flesh and bones! All those "people" we refer to as our colleagues, friends, acquaintances, and even "us" are the same sort of flesh! Can you feel the mere "flesh-ness" of this flesh?

Consider your parents, siblings, friends, colleagues, managers, bus drivers, and anyone else around you in the same way. More importantly, think about yourself in this light. Put yourself in the place of these people and look at yourself from their point of view. Assume that they have read this book and are practicing this exercise about you! Try to look at your body and personal identity through their eyes!

## Returning to the Zero-Point!

If we believe in the existence of entities such as "my self," "my sister," or "my mother," we should seek them somewhere else other than their bodies. "She," if she really does exist, is something else, resides somewhere else, and should be conceived in another manner. The discourse about the nature and definition of the self has been around for a long time. Various thought systems have emerged, based on the answers they have offered to the Question of Self. But perhaps the one thing they all have in common is their attempt to define the self, which has raised ongoing arguments among their supporters.

But let us leave all the presuppositions aside and go further back, to the zero-point. Instead of finding the answer to the question "What is a human?" we must first find out what a human is *not* and what it *cannot be*. One by one, we should omit the entities suggested by any thought system to see what remains in the end! As is the case for any true and genuine research or discovery, the most important priority in this study must be to eliminate incorrect presuppositions and premises.

For thousands of years, the human mind has become used to mistaking the body for the person, but now it is time to break that old habit and see the body as the body, as it is. Having gotten used to mistaking the eyes for the person, the mind now wants to see that the eyeballs are merely a bit of flesh; that is what they really are. The mind has become accustomed to considering the movement of the eyeballs as a person looking in different directions; but it is time to see this as it really is: as the movements of a black or blue or brown or green spot in a ball of fat.

We are constantly watching a horde of moving flesh-and-bone robots, similar to the ones we see in sci-fi movies! Of course, some of these robots might be our friends and relatives, and we ourselves are one of the robots as well!

You might be a salesman, a student, an engineer, or a philosopher, but despite all the complex thoughts you may or may not have had, can you deny that your mind suffers from an odd illusion? An illusion that is above all other illusions? A spell that is above all other spells? An enchantment more amazing than any other?

Confusing a "body" with a "person" is not a trivial mistake. Correcting this mind-made delusion will fundamentally change everything in your view of life. It is not an exaggeration to claim that rectifying this error is prior to any other psychological or self-knowledge discussion. This delusion is mankind's deepest dream, so waking up from it should precede any other awakening. By awakening I mean a sensing and feeling rather than an intellectual realizing of the issue, because a mere logical understanding will not have the destructive effect it should have on the mind's current flawed structure!

However, as mentioned earlier, and as you have probably figured out by now, making the mind realize this logic is not easy, for several reasons. The fact that the mind has to wake up from this hypnotic dream and destroy a deeply rooted habit is not the only problem. The main issue is that the mind suffers from an immense fear and anxiety as soon as it tries to apply this logic. The mind is terrified of this way of looking, to the point that it regards it as its own death. Of course, our "devious" mind is right and discerns the issue correctly. This fear is really justified! One reason behind this fear is the reluctance to face a dreadful loneliness. The mind suddenly realizes that everything it has encountered in life—which has aroused different feelings, including anger, hatred, fear, jealousy, and love—not only has no external existence, but never existed in the first place.

It is as if all the people you have met in life were figures in a painting—figures that you mistook for real. Even more frightening is that your mind has to accept the same fact about itself; it has to realize that it has mistaken a pile of flesh for itself!

There are also other important causes of this fear and resistance. For example, I "need" to keep the images of the people around me as they are in order to be able to release my accumulated hate and anger toward them. I can't just let them go, disappear, vanish, to be forgotten or forgiven! As disgusting as they are, I need them to stay in my mind in order to take my revenge against them sometime in the future. Otherwise, against what can I release this much hate and anger that I am carrying on my shoulders? It is not easy to accept that these despicable identities are the creators of my own mind. It is hard to separate them from their bodies to see those bodies only as bodies, as they are. This is an extremely important topic, to which I intend to return at another time and place. However, you really don't need me to explain this to you. You will soon discover this unpleasant shocking truth by yourself as soon as you start a genuine effort to see the bodies as they are!

## A Voluntary Metamorphosis!

The world in which every person lives exists only for that person. Each mind has its own fabricated world, in which it lives with people of its own creation. Imagine that some people are sleeping next to each other, and each of them is having a dream. Even if they are dreaming about the same thing—for instance, a particular tree—what they see and feel is completely separate from what all the others see and feel. Only the subject of their dreams is the same. To take this example even further, imagine that these people are dreaming about other people in the group. In that dream, let us assume that they are living with each other and talking to each other, not realizing that they are only dreaming each other. Every one of the people in the group is ignorant that the others are also imagining him or her in their self-made

79

dreams and are living with that illusory image, but think they are in contact with physical realities.

It appears that we all live together in a common social or geographical environment. But in reality, it is only bodies—flesh and bones—that are together. The people in those bodies live in their own worlds in absolute solitude. What you live in is an amazing dream. However, no matter how amazing it is, it is still only a dream! Many self-knowledge gurus have noted that human beings have the ability to come out of this deep sleep. In fact, they have emphasized that this is our most important duty as human beings. If we believe that natural evolution is still in progress, it can be claimed that experiencing this awakening will be a decisive and significant mutation in the human evolutionary process. This is going to be a revolutionary evolutionary metamorphosis, which needs to be done individually and voluntarily. No one will do it for us. No one can even start it for us, not even our gods!

# *Part II*

## And the Thought!

Thinking is a complex phenomenon; perhaps, the most complicated operation performed by the brains and minds of the creatures called human. All the issues raised in our discussions so far have been directly related to thinking. How could we expect that relating to the issues discussed in this book is possible without acquiring sufficient experience to observe what is called "thinking"? To better understand the argument of this book, one needs to achieve a tangible sensation of terms such as *mind*, *thought*, *mental space*, and *stream of thinking*.

I have repeatedly noted that the topics discussed here are not philosophical issues to be tackled through abstract reasoning; rather, they should be examined directly through everyday experiences. This discussion leads to fundamental philosophical conclusions, but the way through them is observation, in the sense that one cannot merely rely on thinking and has to observe as well. Therefore, to have an understanding of thought and thinking, let's examine these phenomena through direct observation, without getting trapped into abstract and philosophical arguments.

What is thought and thinking? What do we mean by repeating these words? One could define thinking as a stream of words and images that are produced by the brain or somehow appear somewhere in the mind. Given this definition, when we say that somebody is thinking, we are indicating that a stream of images and words is flowing in the thinker's mind. These mental creations are immaterial entities that are used as arbitrary signs and symbols in the process of thinking. That is, the mind produces abstract representations of real objects and creates a mental construct as a representative of the real World. But the question is, What type of relationship is there between the creatures of the mental world and those of the real external World?

For example, consider the word *water*. In the physical World, water is a substance that can be physically defined and examined. It has physical properties such as volume, temperature, and density, which can be precisely measured. For example, when we say, "The temperature of the water in this container is one hundred degrees Fahrenheit," the addressee grasps what we mean and knows exactly what we are talking about, regardless of the accuracy of the stated information. In other words, exact and specific information is exchanged between the speaker and the listener.

But the situation is not that clear when we consider the water imagined in the mind. First, it is just a word, comprised of a few letters that have no rational reference to real and physical water. Second, it is an abstract symbol with no physically definable properties; for instance, the word *water*, the feeling of water, or remembering water in the mind has no observable physical volume or density or temperature. This "mental water" is merely an abstraction or concept. It cannot even dampen the mental space!

Furthermore, this mental water is imagined differently in different minds. For example, not only are the letters and sounds that produce *water* in English different from those in French, but also the feeling that an English-speaker has toward the word *water* can be different from what a French-speaker feels in his or her mind when hearing or uttering this word. The sense of water is quite different for someone who lives by the sea than for one who lives in the desert. Moreover, this mental feeling can change for a person over time as he or she experiences various events. For example, a long drought would leave a different impression of water in the mind than the one left after a deluge. The example of water can be extended to every other concept that has a physical equivalent; concepts such as wind, fire, journey, money, electricity, mother, father, teacher, and thousands of others.

Therefore, similar words do not necessarily represent similar mental images or similar feelings in different minds. The feelings that each word evokes in the mind are related to a range of factors, such as family situation, environment, geography, culture, society, politics, economy, religion, and so on.

Our mental world—that is, the world in which we really live—which is exactly the same world we feel within us, is a combination of a variety of shifting images, words, and symbols. On the other hand, the external World exists for itself, independent of our mind's activities. My feelings about snow differ from childhood to adulthood to old age. The snow has not changed; it does not care about my feelings; it has its existence independent of me and without being even slightly affected by this chaos in my mind.

Everything out there is like this. The external World is not and cannot be influenced by my mental world or be a function of it. This mental world is the one in which I find myself, and it disappears entirely as soon as my mind stops working for any reason. But nothing changes out there; everything continues to be! What makes this mental world endure is merely the constant flow of my thoughts. It is important to realize the essential difference and distinctness of these two worlds.

## *"Others!"*

Thinking can also be regarded as my mental dialogue with myself or with the images created by my mind—images that I refer to as "others"! We have already discussed these "others" and the essence of their nature! I think it is now a good time for you to try to see the "others" again in the light of this new vision.

## The Stream of Words in the Mental Space

Where do these thoughts and streams of words and images come from? Our thoughts are not in our right ear or left leg. As discussed earlier, our basic feeling is that we have a space in the mind where thoughts—that is, words and images—are produced and streamed. It should be noted that I am using the phrase *mental space* only for purposes of discussion, since it is not comparable to a physical space and lacks its characteristics, such as volume, weight, temperature, and so on. I call it "space" just because that is the way we feel it. But no matter how we may want to define or name this mental phenomenon, we are conscious of it, and we can turn our attention to it. However, we barely use this capacity of paying attention to it and being conscious of it to examine what lies in that space.

We are not concerned here with what other activities may or may not occur in the mind; I prefer to concentrate merely on thoughts and thinking. Even if the question arises, "What is the mind?" my answer would be, "a space where thoughts are produced, comprehended, and felt." A more general answer would be that the mind is the space where the person feels his being and presence. Close your eyes and try to find yourself. Sit in a dark silent place and try to feel the space in which you find yourself, where you sense your "I-ness." This is what I mean by the mental space.

Given our discussion so far, it is clear that we are not referring to what is physically in the actual skull or brain. Basically, this "space" cannot be shown or located; it is a type of sensing and feeling. Its essence lies in us feeling it and is the same as that feeling. It is the specific state in which we find our sense of presence in inner silence. The most noticeable entity that fills this space—if it can be called an entity—is our thought stream. The mind produces thoughts through what is called thinking, and these thoughts fill the mental space. In darkness and silence, I find myself in a vague unknown space that cannot be located, where the most prominent activity is thinking. Right?

## *Self-Awareness!*

"Self-awareness" is the state in which a person is consciously paying attention to his or her mental space, knowing and observing what is going on in there. You may have noticed that we rarely pay attention to what is going on in that space, and are almost ignorant of it most of the time.

The truth is that very few people are in the "state of self-awareness." The majority of us are unaware and ignorant of the contents of our mental space and their activities. It is no exaggeration to say that we are even afraid to look at those contents and activities, and employ various kinds of tools or techniques to narcotize the mind to keep it unaware of its contents and real-time activities. That is why we created the unconscious mind in the first place, and desperately spend a huge amount of energy to keep it unopened in order to avoid directly looking at its contents in a bright light.

91

Probably you have noticed that we are usually not interested in attentively and consciously staying observant of our mental space. Why is it so hard to maintain such an attentive state in real time, the actual time? People say that this is because we have hidden something there which—for some rational or irrational reason—we hate or fear to look at up close with wide-open eyes! Perhaps deep down we know that "thing" is not scary and ugly, but we need to believe it is only because that way of looking at it provides fuel for our hate production machines, a hatred that is used to motivate almost all of our activities. What if all of this horrible game, from beginning to end, is just an illusory self-made dream, which some call the "self"? After the mind knows the trick behind this magic, would it still be difficult for it to stay consciously attentive of its inner space? Or would the mind's natural state be to be aware of everything, without any friction, conflict, or desperation to conceal anything?

There are many valuable texts, some of which go back thousands of years, on the necessity of keeping the mind in an attentive state, or that clarify the reasons behind our lack of interest in maintaining such attentiveness. There is no need to repeat or discuss these arguments here. However, I would like to briefly mention a couple of issues in this regard.

Being aware of thought streams is not an ethical necessity, but rather a rational one. Sound reasoning dictates that human beings should naturally be interested in what is going on in their minds, conscious and aware of this mental space.

Furthermore, awareness is a *must* if you wish to understand the ideas in this book. How can you know the mind without observing its operation? You do realize that mental comprehensions cannot be transferred; that is, we cannot transmit our mental experiences to others. We can just create circumstances so that others can personally experience and comprehend the events. This is certainly not transferring knowledge to another mind, but creating an independent experience in another mind. For example, after I drink a glass of cold water, I cannot transfer my feeling about it to others; I can just provide them with a glass of cold water and ask them to drink it, so they can have their own feeling and understanding. What happens then is their own discovery, not my discovery transferred to them. No one can transfer his or her intuition and experience to you; it is simply impossible.

Only you can be the explorer of your own discoveries! Therefore, in order to understand how your mind works, you have to observe your mental activities yourself. Even if every other human being has found the deepest knowledge and awareness about his or her mind and mental activities, he or she will have added nothing to your understanding of your self. If everyone around you is the best driver ever, not an iota of driving skill will be added to you, unless you sit behind the wheel to learn and practice driving for yourself. Reading hundreds of books about driving will not make you a good driver. Similarly, reading hundreds of books about mind and psyche will not make you a real psychologist or expert on self-knowledge, unless you start to carefully observe your own mind and its activities with the utmost clarity.

This is not an ethical agenda, but a simple logical conclusion, which, fortunately, I doubt anyone denies! You might say it is obvious that no one but me can know my mental space, so why all these explanations and emphases? As I mentioned before, it is because we are not only indifferent toward observing our mental activities, but we actively try to escape from observing them, worrying about the ramifications. Again, the gurus of self-knowledge have discussed this topic in great detail.

## *Observation*

Let me clarify what I mean by observation and what it means to observe the mind's activities and contents. To observe one's own mind does not mean to control it. The word *observation* is used here to mean passive witnessing of what goes on in the mental space at this moment. It does not mean making an active contribution to an interactive activity. We are used to examining our self or the contents of our mind to change something in order to make it better. But that is not the kind of observation I am describing here, and will actually ruin it.

One may think of observation as similar to sitting in a movie theatre and watching what is happening on the screen as it unfolds. This observation is an absolute and pure action of watching without doing or even wanting to do anything. Any active contribution in order to change anything will ruin the quality of this observation. It has to be nothing but watching. Ask yourself why this observation has to be free from any desire to keep things as they are now or to make them different from what they are now. This is simply because it is impossible to see something in real time as it is, and at the same time to try to change it from what it is. If we want to hide something from our sight, or if we want to change it to be different from what it is now, it simply means that we are not able or prepared to look at it yet. Don't you agree?

This way of observing things is not easy; and on your path to self-knowledge, understanding what exactly it means will save huge amounts of your time and energy!

## *"I" Thinks, Therefore I Am Not Yet!*

A self-aware mind is fundamentally different from a non-self-aware one. In the former, an observant agent is watching everything that is going on. In the latter, an observant agent is absent or has a very feeble presence. In a non-self-aware mind, everything is performed "automatically," whereas in a self-aware mind, a silent sense of awareness is attentively observing everything, including automatic procedures. The presence of the observer in a self-aware and self-conscious mind is alive and substantial. This observer is aware that this self-observation is essentially different from thought and thinking, and appears to be beyond them.

In an unconscious mind, there is only the flow of thought streams, one after another, without the mind having any conscious control over them or even paying attention to

97

their essence or duration. As a quick test, can you keep thinking about a topic for five minutes without letting other thoughts invade your mind? Try it now! It is not that simple, is it?

We cannot willingly bring thoughts to mind, nor can we cast them out whenever we wish. Thoughts come and go whenever *they* want, without considering our preferences or even asking for our permission! The stream of thinking keeps moving from one topic to another without our conscious attention. A thought is drawn to a topic by itself, then it focuses on another topic, and then concerns itself with yet another topic, again all by itself. Even when a person believes that he or she has changed the course of thinking, it was the stream that has really been the actual director behind the shift.

For people who are inattentive to thought processes, these issues may seem to be abstract philosophizing and playing with words. But for people who have continually observed their mental activities, these are familiar factual experiences.

When the observer of mental activities is absent, one identifies himself (or herself) with a specific thought as soon as it appears in the mind. To get a better picture of this process, imagine that a few thoughts enter and exit your mind one after the other. When the first thought comes or is being activated, you feel that you are the agent of that thought. The second thought comes and, again, you feel that you are the "thinker" of this second thought. In other words, you feel that you are the first thinker who is now thinking the second thought. But is this correct? Are we really the thinker of our thoughts, or is this just another of the mind's illusions?

First of all, I am not the one who evokes the first thought; nor do I evoke the second. Each thought comes and goes, based on mechanisms beyond my awareness and out of my control or will. Secondly, each thought has a complete process and does not need "me" to operate its specific process of coming and going. The thoughts exist, whether "I" exists or not. The "I" that is felt in every thought process, and is felt to be the agent, the thinker, actually has no role in the process. The agency felt by the "I" is an illusion that is rooted in a false belief. If I am truly the one who does the thinking, why am I incapable of *not thinking*? Why am I not able to control and select the kind of thoughts I have? Why can't I even determine the moment and duration of a specific thought that appears in my mind? Why am I utterly powerless regarding the stream of thoughts in my mental space? What kind of an agent is that powerless and incapable?!

The truth is that the feeling of the agency of the "I" in regard to thinking has no logical basis and is merely an illusion. A new "I" is created with every thought and dies or is temporarily retired when that thought is gone! Each thought brings its own "I" with it. A particular "I" is created with and for any thought. There is no "I" in the mind who thinks the thought or shifts from one thought to another.

The sense of continuity concerning the "I" in the mind is an illusion. There is no collective self that thinks consecutive thoughts. The "I" felt in one thought has nothing in common with the "I" in the next thought. These "I's" are strangers to each other and most of the time are in conflict and create internal contradictions!

When the self-conscious observer is absent from the mind, thoughts take the role of "I." Therefore, whenever the process of thinking is interrupted for any reason and by any means, the self-making process is stopped as well. I do not want to start a discussion here about how thinking can or cannot be stopped, since that is not the concern of this book. Instead, I would like to point out two issues that we did not acknowledge earlier, so as not to create unnecessary distractions.

First, we did not discuss how thoughts move from one to another; that is, what the mechanism is behind the first thought changing into the second, and then shifting to the third, and so on. Second, we took it for granted that only one thought exists in the mind at any one time, when actually it is possible that there may be a multitude of thoughts in the mind at each moment, one of which is closer to the surface, and the rest of which are in the deeper and darker layers of the mind.

In an average mind, in which attention and awareness are not developed, all thought processes, decision-making, and every activity performed through thinking take place in an automatic and unaware state. That is, the person lives and works in a mechanical way, meaning that the thoughts pop up and run by themselves. On the other hand, given our discussion so far, the body also is present and works by itself. Both thought and body exist by themselves, work automatically, and do not need an "I" for being and working. The "I" believes that it dominates both the body and the thought and is the same as them, which is not so. The body and thought do not need "I" for continuing to be and to work. The "I" has no control over anything. It comes and goes with every thought. The "I" considers itself to be the owner and absolute agent of everything. However, this is just a multilayered illusion.

Essentially, a human being with an unaware mind is not basically different from a robot. There are limbs that do certain things, thoughts that come and go, and the deluded mind thinks that it is "I" who is thinking, it is "I" who is seeing, it is "I" who is moving this leg, and it is "I" who is lifting that hand. It is blind to the fact that legs walk, hands move, eyes see, and thoughts come and go as they fancy!

This truth also includes all kinds of feelings. For example, the joy of eating a delicious cake is created by the brain and delivered to the "I," which does not have any agency or creative role in this process. It just "consumes" the data provided by the brain. As another example, consider sex and sexuality. What exactly happens during sex as a biological activity? How is the feeling of it formed? How is the feeling of pleasure created in a sexual experience? Is it the "I" who is creating its joy or pleasure? Or is it actually our brain that creates this feeling and offers it to us as pleasure?

In reality, one is totally separated from the pleasure of sex in any sexual activity, from beginning to end. Imagine a man looking at the body of a woman. He experiences a particular feeling in his mind, a pleasure, an excitement, an attraction, a motivation to look more at or to do something with that body. He believes it is he who "pleasures." He feels that the taste of this feeling is from him, attached to him, is part of him, and is his own. But is this right? No, it is not! That feeling is not coming from his "I" or his sense of "I-ness." It is coming from another source.

When you look at that beautiful face, it is not you who "forms" the beauty of that eye or lip or chin. It is your brain that "forms" and "defines" that beauty. Without your brain and its neural networks, you have no idea what is or is not beautiful. Other than saying, "She is beautiful," we should say, "She is 'beautifulled.'" Forming this beauty is a magical trick that our brain has learned during the evolutionary process to fool us! This is a very clear biological fact, isn't it?

Imagine how beauty is formed or defined for cockroaches or lizards! The way they define or see beauty in their beloved ones looks "terribly" different from the way we define or see beauty in a young woman. But that's fine! That's the way that works for their brains to fool them, just as this is the way that works for our brains to fool us.

It is the brain that is responsible for this task, and it does this in a way that is similar to the way a magician does magic—by creating illusions. Our illusionist brain creates that lady and all of her beauty. We just watch our brain's performance, its wonderful magic, and are fooled by its beauty-illusion show. The beauty or physical attraction we see or feel in the opposite gender is not a real thing. It is something absolutely created and defined and formed by the brain, then tagged onto that curvature, convexity, or concavity of those pieces of bone, flesh, and fat!

The above discussion was about what is called sex and sexuality, not love. Regarding love, let's just say you don't love her, she is "loved"! You don't like her, she is "liked"! Fortunately or unfortunately, that is the way it works. This fundamentally changes many things. Think about it!

As a side note, let me clarify that I am not trying to blame or devaluate sexual behavior or activity. It is a natural instinct and a result of the body's evolution, a tool without which we could not survive. To make my point even clearer, I am not trying to ask you to look at sexual behavior as a joyless or pleasure-less activity.

First of all, it is not you who creates that joy, and you also don't have the power to remove the joy from that activity. It is your body and its brain that are responsible for whatever relates to this complex procedure. This is true not only for sexual activity, but for the joy of eating, listening to music, swimming, and any other healthy natural bodily activity.

103

Second, there is no need to "manipulate" any natural healthy bodily behavior to connect to what I am discussing in this book. In order to follow my argument, "observation" is the only important and necessary exercise that one needs to practice.

It is essential to understand, to observe, and to experience this "separation" of the "I" from whatever belongs to the body. So long as one has not felt his (or her) presence in the mental space, and so long as one has not learned to practice the skill of observing the internal mental activities, it is merely his thought that actually lives, not his self. With this lack of self-awareness, thought takes the place of self. More precisely, the person imagines that his being is the same as his thoughts. He thinks that he exists because his thoughts exist. He mistakenly regards the stream of thinking as the collectivity of the self!

It is only after realizing a deep sense of "presence" that a person comes alive and into being—as if he did not exist before, and it is only now that he has come to life. At this moment, astonished, he will ask himself, "Who was the one that has been living in me so far and has owned my body and psyche?" It is only at this moment, after feeling that presence, that one vividly feels for the very first time the absence and non-beingness state he has been in so far. This is somehow similar to the difference between the quality of real physical sex and what one may experience in masturbation. Let me explain why I say that,

Masturbation is a fake, untrue, and ludicrous mental activity that one performs to delude himself (or herself) into believing that some mind-created imaginary scenes are real. Compared to this, a bodily sexual activity is a physical, real, and genuine behavior for which the mind does not need to do anything other than consciously surrender to the natural flow. In natural physical sex, one does not need to imagine anything to keep the process alive. Instead, the whole body and all of its senses will be involved, and they know how to do their job in harmony, so long as you do not interfere with the natural procedure. As is true for any other genuine activity—such as eating, dancing, listening to music, and so on—thinking can only ruin the joyful feeling of real physical sex by interfering with the natural flow. Contrarily, in masturbation almost everything is done by the mind, so basically it can be described as the mind making love with itself! It is essentially different from the genuine activity performed by two physical bodies when all their physical senses are actively and harmonically involved. As a side note, even when one is involved in physical sex, but uses the mind and imagination to motivate the body to do things, I would describe this as masturbation rather than as genuine sex.

Having said all this, I believe that it should be clear by now why I say that the difference between living in presence and living in absence is similar to the difference between real physical sex and masturbation. After practicing self-awareness and feeling the sense of presence, one realizes

105

that, up to now, he has not been living life, but rather *masturbating* life!

I would like to emphasize that I am not discussing these topics from an ethical perspective. Basically, this discussion is not in the same category as "think positively" or "love thy neighbor as thyself." By saying this, I do not mean to deny or oppose what is called morality or religion. I only intend to clarify that our discussion is not based on ethical points of view; it is logical and—more importantly—experiential. In other words, this argument can be experienced without any need for ethereal explanations, philosophical justifications, or religious and metaphysical beliefs. For example, in order to know the effect that water has on quenching thirst, you just need to drink the water. To know that fire burns the skin, you only have to put your hand in the fire. We do not use ethical, philosophical, or religious arguments in such cases—not because we necessarily have a problem with the arguments, but because the issue at hand is an empirical one that can only be realized through experience.

Another important reason for stating so emphatically that our discussion is not about ethics was implicitly stated earlier. That is, we are not concerned here with the type or nature of the contents of the mind, but rather with observing these contents as they are in order to understand what is going on there. In ethical discussions, the goal is to modify the mind's contents to conform to a specific ethical or religious system; but that is not our aim in this discussion. For instance, the immediate goal here is not to practice

106

observation in order to change hatred into love, or stinginess into generosity. Instead, the first step here is to practice *passive* observation because we understand that willing to change the mind's contents makes it impossible to practice genuine observation. In fact, it will ruin it.

Imagine that someone randomly pops up in my mind at a certain moment, a process that usually happens unconsciously and is beyond my intention or control. Depending on who this person is, a range of diverse feelings may be evoked in my mind. For example, recalling my son or daughter evokes a different feeling from the one that is evoked when I recall my uncle, a neighbor, Abraham Lincoln, or Vincent van Gogh. These feelings can range from love and respect to hatred, rivalry, inferiority, superiority, or many other possibilities. When I maintain that ethics are irrelevant to my discussion, I mean that I am not focusing on ways to control or modify these feelings, but just wanting to see what is going on there.

To attain self-knowledge, we have no way other than to open the unconscious box of the mind and look at its contents under the light of awareness. It is pointless to try to do anything else first. What do you want to do with your mind when you don't yet know what it is made of, how it works, and why it works this way or that way? No one else can do this for you, simply because there is no way for them to get into that land and do this discovery for you. Even if we imagine that someone has access to that space, he or she cannot do this for you. No one can take your self and exercise your self-awareness on your behalf. Genuine gurus know that self-knowledge emerges only after one consciously realizes a crystal clear self-awareness. No tool, no drug, no human being, and no god can help you on this path. Nothing can replace your own self-awareness.

## Impossible to Explain!

An aware mind, one that is conscious of itself, essentially differs from a mind that is ignorant of its contents and behavior. Even if these two kinds of mind share common contents—negative thoughts, for instance—they are quite different. The difference becomes clear *only* to those who have insisted on being passively observant of their mental activities. This difference arises from the actual presence of an observer in a conscious mind. This observer lacks life and presence in an inattentive mind, a mind that is not consciously aware of itself. Such a mind, even if it belongs to a prominent philosopher or psychologist who has done tons of research on the topic, has no concept of such an entity.

Regardless of how much knowledge an inattentive mind may possess, it is in a state of absence. As we noted earlier, it is not possible to explain to other people the difference between this absence and presence. Only after experiencing the presence can one realize the absence. Of course, logically, this is inevitable, since no other option is imaginable. It is only after that moment of epiphany that one realizes he or she has spent a whole lifetime in absence and has actually never existed before! At that specific moment, the phrase *I am* bears a significantly different meaning.

This should not be regarded as an exceptional communication problem between human beings. We can list many other similar communication problems. For example, it is absolutely impossible to explain the difference between red and green to a person who has been blind since birth. Actually, it is impossible to explain this difference, even for people who can see these colors. The only way for a blind person to understand the difference between red and green is to obtain a working visual system. Then he or she will see the difference between these two colors without needing any help from you, not even a single word. Right?

## *My Apologies!*

It might be said that this book has left almost nothing for you. First, it snatched away your eyes, then your ears, and finally your whole body. You no longer see, hear, move, or even breathe! You no longer have an individual, unified, continual thinking self, or any ground to stand on. You have even lost your friends and relatives, in whose place you have received pieces of bone and flesh! Sadly, if you are a man, you may never again be able to enjoy watching beautiful women! And if you are a woman, you may not take pride and pleasure in being the object of men's gazes. Even the taste of an amorous kiss has been lost. How far are those fiery kisses from the contact of pieces of flesh covering pieces of bone!

In principle, I believe that whoever contemplates the issues raised in this book can no longer hold their previous views of the self and the human body. The depth and pace of being influenced by this discussion will differ from one person to the next, but self and body will have a different meaning for the readers of this book as soon as they start to seriously think about the questions asked in this text.

## But Is "The End" That Dismal and Sad?

No, it is not. The end of this story is neither dismal nor sad. As has been stated time and again by knowledgeable masters of self-knowledge, it is only after we deeply comprehend this groundlessness and experience this nothingness that we can apprehend the essence of our being. Only then can we achieve the deepest meanings and the most genuine and worthwhile spiritual experiences.

Furthermore, the gurus have also made it clear that the mind does not actually lose anything after breaking away from the illusions we have discussed in this book. In other words, everything remains the same, and only the way of looking has been fundamentally transformed. Like it or not, according to the sages of self-knowledge, any spiritual understanding that we attain before we experience this nothingness is neither genuine nor authentic. At best, it is contaminated with illusion and fantasy.

There is nothing more serious, necessary, or beneficial than human beings discovering how deep their illusion of self is. In the future, I will discuss how the understanding of this illusion of self can alleviate or even solve many fundamental personal and social predicaments. I have not discussed this issue here, but I understand that I owe it to the readers of this book.

## *About the Author*

Mr. Sanei created the first draft of this work in 2001. For more than thirty-five years, Mr. Sanei has studied the thought systems of most of the major figures in the field of self-discovery and has contemplated self-knowledge. He has also examined a variety of meditation techniques and methods of hypnotism and self-hypnotism.